Endorsements

180 Your Life is like finding a compass for the uncharted territories that come from losing a loved one. As a widow, I worked through the pages of this guide, and I applied the practical life principles you will find at the end of each chapter. It was transformative! If you have experienced loss, then grab this book and allow the pages to chart your course to healing and restoration.

—Julie Stewart Griffis
widowed 10 months, Mother of 3

As a Pastor, I find this book to be the best resource on grieving and overcoming emotional and spiritual pain. Mishael provides tools for healing as well as a practical plan to effectively move forward. This book is a must-read for anyone experiencing the deep pain of loss. I recommend 180 Your Life as the best curriculum for any small group dealing with grief and healing.

—Dan Plourde
Senior Pastor, Calvary Church Jupiter Beach, Florida

As a ministry leader, it truly excites me to be able now to give my grieving people this empathetic compass as a year-long guide after trauma. Mishael Porembski speaks like a seasoned sister, who has been where no one would choose to go and charted a powerful path through the treacherous terrain of devastating loss. As practical as it is poetic, this curriculum not only inspires, but insists on hope. It's a compassionate but firm hand that strengthens every part of the grief-stricken life, including finances, fitness, and friendships. It's real. It's raw. And it's brilliant in a way that begs the question, "Why hasn't anyone thought of this before?"

—Elisabet Fountain
Calvary Chapel Miami Beach Women's Ministry Leader, Author of Come, Fill The Gap

180 Your Life is an authentic perspective of how challenging dealing with the sudden and unexpected loss of a spouse can be. Mishael takes the reader on her own personal journey to the depths of depression and then shares her inspirational story of how she was able to regain her passion for life and even find more purpose than before the tragedy. This is a must-read book for anyone dealing with losing a spouse as well as those who are close to someone who has recently gone through such grief.

—Mike Wien
Founder & President, Specific Edge, LLC and Vice President of the Board for USA Triathlon, the governing body for triathlons within the United States Olympic Committee

Time does not heal all wounds. It just gives you a few more seconds before the loss begins again each day. How is it possible to rebuild from so much grief? Mishael Porembski survived this harsh, tilted world and will show you the way out. Her book is a blueprint for something you need as badly as rebuilding — a cry of joy and not pain.

—Bob Dotson
New York Times Best-Selling Author of American Story, a Lifetime Search for Ordinary People Doing Extraordinary Things

The greatest stories are shaped by our most challenging moments. Mishael is an example of great triumph after tragedy. You will be inspired by her resilience and reminded of our call to love and care for widows and the bereaved in our community. I believe in Mishael and her important message.

—Jeff Shinabarger
Founder of Plywood People and Author of More or Less:
Choosing a Lifestyle of Excessive Generosity

Mishael has opened her heart, her soul, her grief, in order to serve you and me. She describes her "epic, emotional disaster" with humility and humor. If you are experiencing your own trauma, or know someone who is, this book is a must-read. It is a beautifully practical work of love, and is filled with helpful insights and information.

—Robert Fountain
Founder and Senior Pastor of Calvary Chapel Miami Beach, Chaplain
with the Miami Division of the FBI and the Miami Beach Police Department

180 Your Life's year-long grief empowerment plan provides a practical, healthy roadmap to recovery from trauma or loss. Mishael presents the wisdom needed to restore a healthier order to this sacred time of grief. I strongly recommend this beautiful work. It's an incredible read.

—Amy Billingsley, MS, LPC
Covenant Counseling and Consulting

Mishael Porembski allows us into her journey through one of the greatest tragedies in life—that of losing a spouse. I longed for someone to understand the depth of my pain, and to give me hope for the days ahead. Mishael provides the guidance and direction needed to survive grief and to ultimately turn tragedy into triumph.

—Lori McNamara
Widowed 15 months, Founder of 320 Ministries International

I joined Widow Strong seeking friendship with women who understood my grief. Being a part of such a supportive group was life-changing for me. 180 Your Life is the blueprint of positive steps that really worked to strengthen the widows of our team and help us craft a fun and adventurous "New Normal."

—Natalie Simmons
Army widow 12 years, Mother of 3 sons, and one of the original members of Widow Strong

180 Your Life from Tragedy to TRIUMPH: NEW BEGINNINGS

10-Week Personal Study Guide and Journal

A HEALTH, HOPE, AND HEALING GRIEF EMPOWERMENT PROGRAM

By **Mishael Porembski**

With Dr. Larry Keefauver

XULON PRESS

Copyright © 2022 by 180 Your Life, LLC

180 Your Life from Tragedy to Triumph: A Woman's Grief Guide
Personal Study Guide & Journal
By Mishael Porembski with Dr. Larry Keefauver
Edited by Bridget T. Heneghan, Ph.D.

Printed in the United States of America.

Paperback ISBN-13: 978-1-6628-4432-4
Ebook ISBN-13: 978-1-6628-4433-1

Cover photo from Adobe Stock: AdobeStock_69756723
Mishael Porembski's author photo by Atlanta-based photographer Matt Sims of City Light Productions. (GoCityLight.com)
Front cover compass graphic by Loveleen Kaur of Kaazuclip (Creativemarket.com/Kaazuclip)

Back cover design by Michele Slobin at Gryphon Design Strategy (www.gryphondesignstrategy.com)
www.xulonpress.com

Disclaimer

This book contains the opinions and ideas of its authors. It is solely for informational and educational purposes and should not be regarded as a substitute for professional medical treatment. The nature of your body's health condition is complex and unique. Therefore, you should consult a health professional before you begin any new exercise, nutrition, or supplemental program, or if you have questions about your health.

Neither the authors nor the publisher shall be liable or responsible for any loss or damage allegedly arising from any information or suggestion in this book.

Any similarity between the names and stories of individuals described in this book to individuals known by the readers is purely coincidental.

The statements in this book about consumable products or food have not been evaluated by the Food and Drug Administration. The authors or publisher are not responsible for your specific health or allergy needs that may require medical supervision.

Any recipes in this book are to be followed exactly as written. The authors and publisher are not responsible for any adverse reaction to the consumption of food or products that have been suggested in this book.

While the authors have made every effort to provide accurate telephone numbers and Internet addresses at the time of publication, neither the publisher nor the authors assume any responsibility for the errors or the changes that may occur after publication.

Other books from the 180 Your Life series:

180 Your Life from Tragedy to Triumph: A Woman's Grief Guide

180 Your Life New Beginnings: 10-Week Facilitator's Guide for Small Group Study

180 Your Life New Beginnings: 10-Week Video Series

180 Your Life from Tragedy to Triumph: 12-Month Facilitator's Guide

180 Your Life from Tragedy to Triumph: 12-Month Personal Study Guide & Journal

180 Your Life from Tragedy to Triumph: 12-Month Video Series

Learn more at 180YourLife.com

Proceeds from our **180 Your Life** print and video grief empowerment curricula help support our sister nonprofit, Widow Strong. Learn more at WidowStrong.com

Special thanks to my wonderful daughters, Arie and Sophia, for being spectacular warrior women and for always encouraging me to follow my dreams! It's my honor to be your mother! Huge thanks to Pastor Ron Wean, LPC and Pastor Greg Griffin, BCPC for their generous assistance in formatting this 10-week edition. Thanks to graphic editor Joey Garza for formatting the cover of this book. Heartfelt thanks as well to friend, fellow widowed leader, and pastor of spiritual formation, Donna Whitten, at 12 Stone Church for her friendship and insight. I also appreciate the leadership at 12 Stone Church Central Campus in Lawrenceville, GA and their Widow Strong: Steel Magnolias Chapter for testing our New Beginnings 10-Week Grief Empowerment Program. Your team of soulful and sassy widows is more fun and fabulous than I could possibly imagine! Proceeds from this program help support Widow Strong, a 501c3 nonprofit, that empowers widows and their children after loss.

Warrior On, Friends!

Mishael

How to Use This Study Guide–From Mishael

S et aside time on a regular basis to go through the book and do the activities given in this study guide. This program is designed to be an overview of the 8 Steps for Grief Empowerment found in the original 180 Your Life – 12 Month print and video grief empowerment series. This study guide and journal pairs directly with the book 180 Your Life from Tragedy to Triumph: A Woman's Grief Guide. There are chapter assignments to read for each section. *If you would rather listen to the chapter readings, please search for "180 Your Life" on Audible.com for the audiobook version of the main book read by me, the author. For additional free resources for this program, visit 180YourLife.com/ free-resources.*

In this program, you can find powerful tools for your grief journey. There is no "magic pill" to make it all better; it will be your time, prayer, and wise decisions that directly craft a life you love.

The journal questions are designed to spark mindful thoughts so that you can assess your *current* life, create healing solutions, and craft peace in your environment. You don't have to answer all the journal questions, but they are the questions that helped me to process and heal from my loss, so give it a shot.

It is ideal to have an accountability/prayer partner, *and p*referably, someone who is at a different level of grief processing than you are.

Grief *and* our transformation *don't* happen on our timetable. As you lean into loss, my prayer is that you discover the amazing adventure God has for you and your life's purpose. Trust the process and His providence. Let's do this!

Be the Light,

Mishael

Week 1

Worksheet for Preparation
Introduction

Read Preface and Introduction
180 Your Life from Tragedy to Triumph

As you read the preface & introduction of the book, what words did you also think of that might describe the aftermath of loss?

The author shared that she desperately needed to know that she and her family would really survive this loss and that someone really understood what they were going through. She said she also needed someone who knew how to successfully slog through the broken dreams and come out whole on the other end.

The author personally walked this path and desires to help you successfully navigate your way through as well.

One of the most transforming moments for the author at her own Ground Zero was when someone she called a "pay it forward widow" came to her home a few weeks after her husband Jason died.

As you read about this "pay it forward widow," what descriptive words stood out to you about her?

Would you like to meet a person like this who was open, honest, and transparent with her own story of grief? Why or why not?

Have you found such a person in your life?

Who could help mentor you in this process?

What can you do to meet an inspirational, empowered person in your area of loss who could act as a mentor in your life? (Hint: try finding a support group in your area.)

Start keeping a journal and record your thoughts as you read each chapter. Before Week 2, please read Chapters 1-4 in the book, "180 Your Life, From Tragedy to Triumph." If you are pressed for time, you can opt to listen to the audible version of the main book by purchasing a copy of "180 Your Life" on Audible.com, read by the author, Mishael Porembski.

As you begin this journey, ask God to be your guide. Make a commitment to meet with Him each day and allow Him to minister to you as you journey to sunrise.

Food for Thought

Week 1: Journal Entries

Welcome! You have made a huge step by deciding to complete the 180 Your Life program! I'm so honored and so proud of you! Let's take a little time this week to figure out where you are on your journey. ~ Mishael

Day 1: Where are you on your journey?

Food for Thought

Week 1: Journal Entries

Day 2: How do your mind, body, and spirit feel?

Are you dry like the desert or do you feel life beginning to grow?

Food for Thought

Week 1: Journal Entries

Day 3: If you are dry, where are the dry areas in your life?

Food for Thought

Week 1: Journal Entries

Day 4: Where are the green areas in your life?

Food for Thought

Week 1: Journal Entries

Day 5: Go have some fun with your family and write about what you did.

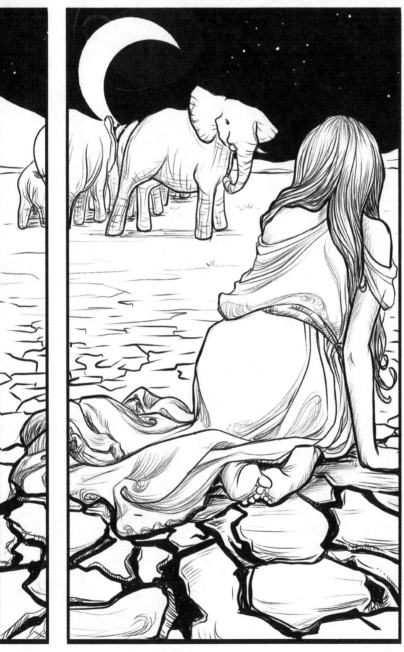

Empower your Ground Zero

Week 2

Worksheet for Step 1
Empower Your Ground Zero

Read Chapters 1-4
180 Your Life from Tragedy to Triumph

B efore you begin, take a moment to talk with God. Ask Him to be your personal guide as you go through this chapter and study. Be open and honest with God and yourself about how you are feeling. Allow Him to minister to you as you read this chapter and process all that He is doing in your life.

Chapter 1: Ground Zero Worksheet

At times, Christians want to quickly put a "bow" on massive tragedy and find purpose in the pain. However, the author transparently shares that she did not want anyone to try to make this okay. She didn't want to hear about how all things work together for good—not at that moment.

Raw grief is such an affront to all that seems right. It's messy and even distasteful. It is waves of sobbing mixed with moments of rage. It feels like a tornado flattening your home, ripping through the roof, breaking glass, and throwing everything around. It feels out of control.

Have you or are you still experiencing times of "raw grief" that feel like that raging tornado?

How did most people around you react to those raw grief times?

The Bible talks about grieving with those who grieve. That is a scary emotional place to go, but it's also one of the deepest gifts you can give a loved one who is grieving.

What does it mean to grieve with those who grieve?_____

Did you have someone like the author did who did this for you?

How would you advise someone to grieve with someone who is grieving? What were some of the things the author's friend, Michael, did for the author?

Look up the Jewish tradition of "sitting Shiva," which comes from the story of Job. What insights did you learn from this tradition that help you in your grief journey?

Read Job 2:11-13. When Job lost his home and children, his friends came to grieve with him, and for the first seven days, they just sat silently with him in the dust. There was nothing to say to make it better.

How would you describe Job's grief?

How did Job's friends mourn with him after his tremendous loss?

The author's friend was simply present. What did that mean?

What lesson did you learn from this Jewish brother about how to grieve with those who grieve?

No matter what the loss you have suffered, there is more to it than just being the surviving loved one. Answer these questions based on what the author shared.

In what areas do you need courage while you are grieving?

What were some of the ways you had to protect yourself during this time?

When you were in the initial stages of grieving, did you experience "emotional drunk driving?" Describe one of those times.

Review: Journey to the Sunrise

Do not be surprised when families fight, reject us, or drop out of our lives during the grieving period because those who are grieving are basically "drunk driving" when it comes to their emotions.

How did you experience this?

Realize grief does not always bring out the best in us. It can make us react in ways we never thought possible.

How did you react?

Understand that you must give grace where you can and protect yourself when necessary.

Describe a time you had to give grace. How would you handle the situation if you had it to do over?

Practical Suggestions for Transforming Trials into Triumph

Focus on the moments of grace during the storm, like a special dish someone cooks, the presence of friends, those who step up to help provide food, clean your house, and mow your lawn.

List some of those gifts of grace.

People don't truly know what to say in the face of such a train wreck of the soul, so allow them to lend helping hands and comfort in the little ways designed to help you navigate those first few days.

Make up a list of suggestions that you can give to someone who wants to help a friend who is going through these initial stages of grieving.

Ask God to remind you of those times of grace and to help you learn wisdom in protecting yourself as you move into your new life without your deceased loved one.

Remember to write what you gleaned from this chapter and your thoughts in your journal.

Speak Life
Empower Your Ground Zero

(Read Out Loud)

I will not lie down in the Desert of Grief. That is not my destiny. I am on a quest. Though the grasses have browned, the ground has cracked, and the night is full of the unknown, I sense a presence. I ask God to show me the way to the flood lands of the soul. I rise, taking one step and then another, moving forward into the night, pressing on toward the waters of renewal and the light of day.

Food for Thought

Week 2: Journal Entries

Day 1: Your Ground Zero Story

This is going to feel intense for a little while, but hold on, Sister! We have to survey the situation before we can clean up and build. ~ Mishael

This part could be hard to write, but it's important to express your loss. What's your Ground Zero story?

Food for Thought

Week 2: Journal Entries

Day 2: Taking Stock

What were you doing the day your life changed? How did you find out?
What happened after you found out?

Food for Thought
Week 2: Journal Entries

Day 3: Burning Questions

What are the unanswered questions from your loss?

Food for Thought

Week 2: Journal Entries

Day 4: Ask God

What are the questions you want to ask God about your loss and circumstances?

Food for Thought

Week 2: Journal Entries

Day 5: Anchor in the Ocean

Even if God never gives you the answers you seek, can you still choose to trust Him?
What is your "anchor" verse for this time? Mishael's was, *"In my anguish I cried to the LORD, and he answered me by setting me free"* (Psalm 118:5 NIV).

Week 3

Worksheet for Step 2
Forge Your Team

Read Chapters 5-7
180 Your Life from Tragedy to Triumph

In the book, the Blacksmith said when he re-attached the two pieces, soldering them together by adding part of a melted steel rod, that the resulting piece was "Stronger than before." Why do you think this is true?

How has this proven true in your life?

The author was transparent when she said,

> *"God and I were not on good terms after Jason died. I felt bitter and angry for no short amount of time. The bitterness and anger came with a host of other emotions, such as numbness, terror, guilt, loneliness, and depression."*

How do you relate to these feelings? Were yours constructive or destructive?

What things did you use to try to outrun your pain?

Mishael writes,

> *"Looking back, I wonder if the emotions that invaded me might have been the tools used to reshape me."*

Do you see how this could be true in your own life?

Chapter 5: Ground Zero Posse

In the early days, therefore, you must harness the goodwill that is so plentiful. Here's a secret: your friends and neighbors want to do something to help. If you allow them to help once, and they feel successful, they will want to help again. Your friends care about you, and they need to *exercise* their feelings of grief, sympathy, relief, and guilt. You give their grief a purpose by asking them for specific, concrete help.

Your need can be a gift to your friends and neighbors; you are offering them a chance to feed their spirits. You also open the door for your new Team—those among your acquaintances who are uniquely equipped to usher you through your transition.

Think of those who were part of your emotional posse.

What stories do you have of how people around you have helped you through?

How was it difficult for you to allow these people to help you?

What were the benefits of letting those God sent you help you walk through your grief?

How did what they did for you give you hope that in time you would be healed?

Practical Support: Designate an Organizer

The first step in getting help is knowing what types of help you will need. The second is *realizing* that people want to help. The third is asking for it.
If you have not already done so, make these lists in your journal this week.

o   *What type of help do you need?*
o   *Who are the people who have said they want to help?*
o   *Who have you asked to help?*

Who did you find as an organizer to help you with making those tough and everyday decisions?

Can you get help executing some tough decisions among the individual support of several friends or family members (spread the load)?

What benefits did you receive from following this good advice?

Mishael writes,

> *"When I began my grief journey, I simply flew on autopilot and tried everything that came to mind in order to cope with my new condition. Afterward, I had to clear away the rubble of these efforts in order to create the life I could love once again. With the benefit of hindsight, however, I can offer some suggestions for someone who is facing loss."*

Points to remember

1. You need people around you because even simple tasks can feel overwhelming when you are in grief. The extra energy brought by having friends alongside you is important.

2. You may have to be proactive and organize friends for yourself.

3. If you have a family member or a friend who is willing to act as your secretary and bodyguard during the first week, then pin him or her with an official title. This person need not be a best friend, but rather someone who is tactful, firm, organized, and—most importantly—willing.

Who can be this person in your life?

The Organizer's job duties are:
- First, take down the names, contact information, and skill sets of those wanting to help.
- Second, have these volunteers commit to a schedule of help.
- Third, run interference for you when you are in the midst of meltdowns.

On signupgenius.com, you or your organizer can email the link to all the friends and neighbors who want to help, and they can view the schedule and sign up for specific tasks on specific days. Other useful volunteering websites are volunteergenius.com and caringbridge.org.

The organizer should also make a list of all the items given to the grieving family and write the thank you notes, leaving the signature area blank for you to sign.

Ideally, your Posse will consist of several key Go-To People, in charge of:

1. Finances
Who is this person?

Why is this important?

What suggestions would you give someone else?

2. Food
Who is this person?

Why is this important?

What additional suggestions would you give?

3. Home Care
Who is this person?

Why is this important?

What other suggestions would you offer?

4. Exercise
Who is this person?

Why is this important?

What other suggestions could you also give about this?

5. Activities
Who is this person?

Why is it so important?

How would you help someone else?

6. Organizations
What church groups, small faith groups, and volunteer groups such as FloodStudentMissions.org did you find helpful?

Mishael writes,

> *"My best advice is to ask for help as often as you need it—don't save up requests or postpone your needs, but also, respond with grace and gratitude whenever someone cannot help at the moment."*

Identify Your Posse

Life marches on. It's inescapably true. You want it all to stop, but it just doesn't. Kids still have to eat, lawns will grow, laundry will get dirty, and you will have to establish kind and firm bound- aries to honor your life and home environment. Don't be afraid to speak up and take the reins when necessary. It will feel tough sometimes. Some folks may not take kindly to it at first. That's okay. Don't be afraid to stand firm as the leader in your life and home.

Meditate on the verse:

"Have I not commanded you? Be strong and courageous. Do not be afraid; do not be discouraged, for the LORD your God will be with you wherever you go" (Joshua 1:9 NIV).

Review: Journey to the Sunrise

Do not be surprised when life marches on.

Realize that you may have to speak up and stand up as the leader of your life.

Understand that you need to ask for help as often as you need it.

Pray and ask God to surround you with those who will help you as you walk through this journey. Write your prayers here.

Speak Life
Forge Your Team

(Read Out Loud)

As I press into this journey, I will join others who understand my loss around the campfire, so we may strengthen one another for this quest. We will come together in trust and confidence, for protection, friendship, and renewal. We will speak hope, speak purpose and speak life to one another. Though the plains are arid, we take refreshment at a watering hole, encouraging one another, content to know we are not alone.

Food for Thought

Week 3: Journal Entries

Day 1: The Blacksmith

Purpose to look for God in your circumstances. Be honest with God. He can handle it. Pour your heart to Him. It's also time to be proactive and start empowering your circumstances by engaging your posse of helpers. ~ Mishael

Can you, like a camera, "zoom" out from your pain in the middle of the fire and see the larger picture? What does that look like right now?

Food for Thought

Week 3: Journal Entries

Day 2: Do you see God at work?

If you cannot see God at work yet, can you trust that God is working anyway? Can you trust that God is using the fire of grief to transform you? Write out your heart's thoughts.

Food for Thought

Week 3: Journal Entries

Day 3: Tell God how you feel about Him

It's okay to be real. Honesty is the bedrock of trust. Meditate on this verse. What does it mean to you? *"Fear not, for I am with you; Be not dismayed, for I am your God. I will strengthen you, Yes, I will help you, I will uphold you with My righteous right hand." (Isaiah 41:1)*

Food for Thought

Week 3: Journal Entries

Day 4: Ground Zero Posse

Make a list of things that you need help with now and in the coming months. Think about areas like the interior of the home, the exterior of the home, yard work, repairs, food, paperwork, and so on.

Make a list of your friends and family and their areas of expertise. Who could you ask to help you with specific tasks?

How can you help them in return?

Food for Thought

Week 3: Journal Entries

Day 5: Enlist someone to help you organize helpful steps

Who is that person and what can you achieve together? Pray for them, giving thanks for who they are in your life.

Week 4

Worksheet for Step 2
Train Your Mind

Read Chapters 8-10
180 Your Life from Tragedy to Triumph

Chapter 8:

Bargaining with Grief

What are the five stages of grief?

    1.

    2.

    3.

    4.

    5.

Look these up online and develop a definition for each one. Write it out above.

At first, you are too steeped in sorrow to realize that the loss that has changed your family dynamics has also changed your social dynamics.

How did the death of your loved one affect and change your social status?

Grief can punch other holes in your everyday life as well. You find yourself avoiding places that hold memories of your loved one. You abandon the activities that once took up part of your day, because you had been doing them for another's sake, like cooking a full meal, or exercising, or dressing up. The incentive is gone. Now, as you view this enormous crater that seems to be expanding before your eyes, you try to fill it up.

What were some of the ways you used to fill up that crater left by your loss, trauma, or the death of your loved one?

What choices were constructive? Why? What choices were destructive? Why?

Mishael writes,

    "One day it hit me. I was being constricted out of my own life.

"I wasn't moving freely, and, what was worse, it was slowly killing my soul. My fear was slowly affecting my children and their lives, too. While the grief constrictor was slowly squeezing away the possibilities for joy, movement, and even choices in my life, I was busy drowning myself in the debris of distractions."

Have you been drowning yourself in the debris of distractions? Explain.

What has this done to your life and the lives of those closest to you?

Mishael continues,

"I calmly and firmly took hold of the situation.

I purposely unwrapped the constrictor from around me."

How are you doing this in your life?

What choices are you going to make this week to unwrap the constrictor from your life? Name up to three choices.

How would you help someone else going through this phase of grief?

Training for the New Normal

Be aware that the constrictor comes in different forms.

It can take the shape of any emotion that inhibits life, like depression, fear, unforgiveness, resentment, or anger. The constrictor can also come as a craving for something that isn't good for you—in Mishael's case, too much sugar. You want so badly to dull the pain, and the constriction is so subtle, that you hardly notice it happening.

What emotions began to constrict your life after the death of a loved one?

How would you help someone else dealing with a constricting emotion within her grief?

What craving did you deal with at the various stages of your grief?

Did you handle it constructively or destructively? Explain.

You must take charge because constrictors play for keeps.

What was the secret of effectively establishing your new normal, your new life?

Someone told Mishael, "It hurts to heal." How is this true in your life?

What helped you move forward in spite of the hurt?

Did you experience emotional suffocation? Explain.

Simplify Your Life

One way to feel in control of your environment is to simplify your home, relationships, and life. This is not a quick fix, but in the long run, it makes for a peaceful home life.

What are some of the areas you need to simplify in your life? If you have already begun to do this, how did you do it?

How would you help others do this?

How can you break down your larger goals into weekly and daily tasks?

How can you pair up with an accountability partner to commit to completing these tasks? (Start small and gain success, then tackle a larger goal.)

Pray and ask God to help you begin to train your mind in this area of moving through the bargaining phase of grief. Ask Him to begin to reveal to you your New Normal.

Review: Journey to the Sunrise

Realize that there is power in simplicity.

Understand that it hurts to heal.

Remember to establish order in your environment. You need to simplify your home, relationships, and lifestyle.

Speak Life
Train Your Mind

(Read Out Loud)

I have met the constrictor, which stealthily coiled around me while I grieved, almost imperceptible, threatening to constrict my movements and even my very breath. With courage, asking for God's help, I will take conscious steps to firmly unwrap its coils from my life, minimizing chaos and creating healthy boundaries, as I purpose to create calm and peace in my home and my mind.

Food for Thought

Week 4: Journal Entries

This week we are going to unwrap the constrictor from our lives. Philippians 4:13 says, "I can do all things through the Messiah who strengthens me" (TLV). Get a firm grip behind the serpent's head and let's uncoil it, for our freedom. ~ Mishael

Day 1: Bargaining With Grief: Kathy the Python

In what ways is grief constricting your life?

Food for Thought

Week 4: Journal Entries

Day 2: Uncoil the Snake

What can you do to uncoil this snake from around yourself? (Take some time to pray for God's strength and wisdom.)

Meditate on Galatians 5:1, *"For freedom, Messiah set us free—so stand firm, and do not be burdened by a yoke of slavery again" (TLV).*

Food for Thought

Week 4: Journal Entries

Day 3: Negative Habits

List three negative habits you are using to avoid the pain of grief. What can you do this week to take a step in a positive direction?

Food for Thought

Week 4: Journal Entries

Day 4: Surveying the Suffocation

Are projects and busyness suffocating you out of the time you need to take care of yourself and become mindful of where your life is going?

What can you do to change?

Food for Thought
Week 4: Journal Entries

Day 5: The Bargaining Phase

What are ways you bargain with grief?

Are you avoiding your life as it is today? How?

What can you do to take a positive step in making the most of your life today?

Week 5

Worksheet for Step 4
Train Your Body

Read Chapters 11-13
180 Your Life from Tragedy to Triumph

Chapter 11: God as Coach and Stepping Out of the Well

Mishael shares in the book,

> *"Over the years, I have teetered between various diets and comfort-food comas. I have tried various supplements that were supposed to trick my body into shedding pounds. I have jumped on diet bandwagons and followed complicated recipes with exotic ingredients. The problem is, plunging into these weight-loss schemes was akin to buying the latest storage system for my clutter. Until I actually got rid of the junk, it would always eventually return to overwhelm me. Most of my diet attempts would work for a while—and then stop working."*

Fill in the blanks on these mental steps in order to "180 Your Life."

> *"I had to realize that _____ peace was necessary for _____ peace."*

What does this mean to you?

> *"I realized to release stress, I had to create order to minimize the _____ in my life."*

How did you do that in your own life?

> *"I had to recognize that surrounding myself with things would not create a shield between me and my grief; it would only _____ my _____ and _____. "*

As you did this, how did it help you move forward in your new life?

> *"I had to realize that when I asked friends, neighbors, strangers, and my own children to help, I was _____ and _____ them, not adding to their burdens."*

What are some of the things you have asked others to do to help?

"I had to realize that the simplicity and peace that I sought would have to translate to my _____ and _____ as well."

What did you learn from reading this chapter?

"We know that we can reach the mind through the_____."

"We can purposely alter our moods by changing our _____ or _____."

"If we smile, just forcing the face muscles into the smile position helps us feel more positive and less stressed."

Try this. How did it make you feel?

"If we stand up straight, we will automatically feel more _____ and less _____."

Try this. How did it make you feel?

When You Feel Bad, Look Good!

Mishael writes,

> *"I am often reminded of a story a good friend once told me about a stubborn donkey that had been thrown down a well by his nasty owner. To add insult to injury, the owner proceeded to throw trash on top of the donkey in the well. Each time trash rained down on the donkey, she stepped on top of the trash. The cruel owner didn't realize that with every piece of garbage, the donkey was getting closer to the opening of the well. Finally, the donkey stepped on top of the last piece of trash and then simply stepped out of the well."*

The good decisions we make while we are in the well are the stepping stones for getting out of a bad situation.

What are some of the good decisions you are going to make as a result of reading this chapter?

Fill in the blanks for these key points in this chapter.

Our efforts toward "looking good," our view of the accumulating trash that we have been able to rise above, will inevitably lead to our _____.

When your body is working well and sleeping well, you will feel more _____ and _____

When your body feels empowered, it's easier to make _____, life-affirming decisions during times of grief.

Good food choices give more _____ and _____ better _____.

Achieving success in the _____ realm is a great step in claiming your life as it is today.

Properly _____ your body while you are grieving can help you feel stronger, calmer, and better able to manage your circumstances.

Once you are able to sleep, create strategies to level your blood and calm your nerves, you can _____ life as it is today.

Mishael shares,

> *"It makes sense that a great loss will result in grief—especially the loss of a loved one or of something that played a large role in your everyday life. We are learning that grief not only creates stresses in our bodies that result in chemical and digestive imbalances; it also can be measured by the absence of the hormones that help us feel good while we are in healthy relationships. So, it seems natural that you would want to stimulate those pleasure centers in your brain with an easy fix, like sugar, alcohol, drugs, or smoking. Maybe that's why we all reach for comfort foods in a grief situation. These toxins do stimulate the pleasure centers of the brain, but only temporarily, and with bad side effects."*

As you read the different reasons why not to eat these unhealthy foods, what stood out to you about each one?

What did you learn that you didn't know before about each one?

Alcohol

What stood out?

What did you learn?

What are you doing to eliminate it from your diet? How did you feel after you eliminated it?

Gluten

What stood out?

What did you learn?

What are you doing to eliminate it from your diet? How did you feel after you eliminated it?

Dairy

What stood out?

What did you learn?

What are you doing to eliminate it from your diet? How did you feel after you eliminated it?

Sugar

What stood out?

What did you learn?

What are you doing to eliminate it from your diet? How did you feel after you eliminated it?

Caffeine

What stood out?

What did you learn?

What are you doing to eliminate it from your diet? How did you feel after you eliminated it?

Soda

What stood out?

What did you learn?

What are you doing to eliminate it from your diet? How did you feel after you eliminated it?

Artificial Sweeteners

What stood out?

What did you learn?

What are you doing to eliminate it from your diet? How did you feel after you eliminated it?

Steps on the Path

Take the Nutrition Challenge. Nourishing your body, especially during times of grief, empowers you to feel stronger faster.

Try it for twenty-one days by taking away one food that is bad for you every three days, and see how you feel.

Let your body "reset" nutritionally by making conscious choices to eliminate destructive foods that disrupt your digestion and your body's ability to nourish itself. Instead, take wise steps to strengthen your body for the adventure that lies ahead. Want to get more strategies for a healthful detox? Check out the book *The Hormone Cure* by Sara Gottfried, MD.

A healthy lifestyle is not just about avoiding certain toxins, it's about making good choices.

Review: Journey to the Sunrise

Discover that your state of mind is influenced not only by those things and people around you, but also by what's inside you. Your food consumption and chemistry are an integral part of your healing.

Realize that outer calm is a necessary component for inner peace. Purpose to make wise eating choices.

Understand that achieving success in the physical realm is a great step in claiming your life as it is today.

   Action Step: Check out Appendix 2, Taste of Triumph

Pray and ask God to help you take the nutrition challenge. Thank God for the good food He has provided to nourish your body. Write your prayers here.

Speak Life
Train Your Body

(Read Out Loud)

Even when the sands were hot, I have purposed to strengthen my body through conscious, healthy choices in what I eat and drink. I commit to an exercise schedule in a supportive, accountable Team, with a definite finish line, in order to accomplish my health goals. I will be open to asking God to be my coach.

Food for Thought

Week 5: Journal Entries

We are starting to gear up, Sisters! It's time to rev the engine and empower your body. You can do it, one step at a time! ~ Mishael

Day 1: God as Coach

Are there people or circumstances that hold you back from training?
What can you do to set healthy boundaries so that you can nourish yourself and become stronger?

Food for Thought

Week 5: Journal Entries

Day 2: Ask God to be your coach

Are you reading the "playbook" on a regular basis? (Proverbs is a great place to start.) Take a walk today and just have an honest conversation with God.
Afterward, write about your experience and the thoughts that came to mind.

Food for Thought

Week 5: Journal Entries

Day 3: Exercise and Healthy Eating

What have you done to start your journey to wellness and strength?
Write about how you felt taking your first steps to take care of yourself after loss.

Food for Thought

Week 5: Journal Entries

Day 4: Start Today

How about today?
What have you done, or what will you do today to empower yourself? What exercise do you have planned?

Food for Thought

Week 5: Journal Entries

Day 5: Ask Them Today

Have you found a group to exercise with?
If not, can you ask friends to join you on specific days of the week? Write your thoughts.

Train Your Spirit

Week 6

Worksheet for Step 5
Train Your Spirit

Read Chapters 14-16
180 Your Life from Tragedy to Triumph

Chapter: 14 Kitten Pillow and Learning to Trust Again

Mishael writes,

> *"In that moment, I realized that the way we live matters beyond our time on earth.*

> *"Our suffering and the choices we make during our pain are not only about us, or even about survival of our immediate family—although that is certainly part of the process. From a larger perspective, our choice to have hope, faith, and strength in desperate times may be the example needed by those who will go after us. Those we have never met, that is our living legacy, creating beauty through our padetermining to find hope. That is our own intricately embroidered kitten pillow that we pass on to those we love."*

How did the kitten pillow story help you move forward on your journey?

Have you stopped asking, Why did this happen to me?

Have you started asking, What will I do with this mess?

What have you decided to do with the mess?

In what way can you create beauty from ashes?

Think about creative ways to commemorate important anniversaries.

How can you celebrate the lives of the loved ones you have lost as you come up on the anniversary of their death or other significant anniversaries, like birthdays, holidays, or wedding anniversaries?

What are some creative ways you have celebrated past anniversaries or holidays? What are some ways you would like to celebrate an anniversary or holiday?

Think creatively, dream, and plan something unexpected for you and your family. With that in mind, what could you do differently, or new?

Divine Distrust

Mishael shares,

> *"This would be a much easier book to write if I could tell you that when I found my community, ate healthy foods, and crossed finish lines, everything in my life came into order and my heart was healed. If I said that, I would not be practicing transparency with you. Certainly, my life moved forward dramatically when I found my Team, trained my body and mind, and felt the triumph of crossing finish lines. However, my spirit was still restless, on guard, and on the lookout for danger. Constantly wanting to protect my heart and my children, I was exhausted. Viewed from the outside, I was still going to church, I was still reading the Bible, and praying with my kids. However, I didn't fully trust God again after Jason's death—not really.*
>
> *Minor detail, right?*
>
> *So, what if I didn't fully trust God again after the death of my husband? Seems like we should have the right to hold back a little of our heart after the tragedy of loss, right? Anyway, who is going to detect that? We can hide our sense of Divine Distrust deep within us, right?"*

Why is this assumption wrong?

What does holding onto Divine Distrust do to our lives? What does it affect?

Wounded Horses

If someone gets close enough to your wounds, or if you feel threatened, does your spirit kick and buck, wild-eyed in your dark stable like the story of the wounded horse in the movie mentioned in this chapter? Share your thoughts.

How did the trainer in the movie The Horse Whisperer help the horse overcome its trust issues?

(If you haven't already, watch The Horse Whisperer.)

How has God been helping you overcome your trust issues with Him?

What have you done to appear strong during this time to try and "fool" those around you?

Have you tried to take care of things the best you could by yourself?

How has that worked out for you?

How would you advise others trying to do this on their own?

Mishael writes,

> ***"Eventually, I realized that being mad at God is like a child being angry with a parent."***

Should your anger with God keep you from moving toward Him on your grief journey?

How can you keep moving toward Him even as you deal with your anger toward Him?

Did your anger with God cause trust issues with Him? Explain.

Did you look back over the beginning stages of your grief and see how God has been there with you every step of the way?

How have you been exercising your trust muscles?

Full Stop

From Mishael:

> *"Sometimes God will bring us to a Full Stop in order to humble us and force us to ask others for help."*

Have you ever had to trust God to help you get even the bare necessities completed?

Have you ever had to be in constant dialogue with God, asking Him to provide help at every step?

Have you had to humble yourself and ask others to help you out? Why do you think God put you through that?

List the ways God has come through for you again and again, providing the help you needed just when you needed it.

Have you been afraid to let your guard down just in case God did not show up on time to meet your needs?

How has that worked out for you?

Have you begun waiting on God's timing rather than always moving forward in your own strength? Explain.

How would you help others to move to that level of trust in God?

What was the lesson the author learned through the story of her kitchen make-over?

What happened when the author started to genuinely believe that God loved her and that He was aware of her?

Have you had a similar experience with God? What happened to you?

Review: Journey to the Sunrise

Discover that without finding the spiritual rest that comes from trusting God, you will always be on the run, trying to protect your family, and always spiritually exhausted.

Realize that you must train your spirit as conscientiously as you train your body, mind, and household.

Understand that God will protect and provide for you and your family, but it might not come in the form you expect.

Steps on the Path

Be open to life lessons, and simply start the Divine Conversation.

Take a step to release Divine Distrust because it will affect everything in your life. God is there to help build trust again so He can bring you healing.

With your utter dependence on Him, a shift will begin in your relationship with God. Reading a Psalm from the Bible each day is a great place to start.

Focus on honesty with God, which is the beginning of trust, and gives way to healing and eventually love. This has been the simple prayer Mishael has prayed with her daughters for years now: "God, please heal our hearts and minds and help us to trust You."

Have you been staying connected to God through prayer and reading the Bible daily?

How has this helped exercise your trust muscles?

Have you been training your spirit to praise in spite of whatever your emotions or inclinations demand each day?

How has this helped with your relationship with God?

Pray, asking God to help you begin to deal with your Divine Distrust. Write out your prayers here.

Speak Life
Train Your Spirit

(Read Out Loud)

I have continued to press into the heart of grief when it felt most dry. I have chosen gratitude, forgiveness, prayer, kindness, and generosity of soul in the most parched of circumstances. Even when the grasses around me were flaming hot with the heat of loss, I have purposed to press on, seeking God in prayer, worship, and Bible reading as an act of will. By the grace of God, I will not run from the desert, but instead will make positive choices in the midst of my tragedy, practicing spiritual discipline, which will yield a mighty harvest in due time. I will follow the ancient paths back to God, trusting and believing that the mighty floodwaters of the Spirit will come, the refreshment from the hand of God.

Food for Thought
Week 6: Journal Entries

Taking time to make mindful choices that honor your spirit is a great way to fall in love with your life as it is today. ~ Mishael

Day 1: Inspirational People

Who is an inspirational person in your life? What makes him or her inspirational to you? Write about it.

Food for Thought

Week 6: Journal Entries

Day 2: The Kitten Pillow

Do you know someone who has created beauty from his or her pain? How was it accomplished?

Food for Thought

Week 6: Journal Entries

Day 3: Take some time to pray

Go on a walk if you need to, and think about the ways that you could create beauty from your pain.

Food for Thought

Week 6: Journal Entries

Day 4: It isn't just about you

Who else is influenced by your choices?
How are you coloring their lives with your decisions?

Food for Thought

Week 6: Journal Entries

Day 5: Intentional Honoring

How can you intentionally honor someone you have lost? Write about it.

Cross Your Finish Line

Week 7

Step 6: Cross Your Finish Line
Train Your Spirit

Read Chapters 17-19
180 Your Life from Tragedy to Triumph

Chapter 17: Becoming a Victor, Not a Victim

As you read the author's experience with her daughter in this triathlon race, what beautiful lessons did you learn?

How important is your support group as you move from being a victim to becoming a victor?

How did this object lesson help you frame your life after loss? How does this compare with your race toward heaven?

What does crossing any kind of finish line inspire in your life, especially after a loss?

How did the Stories of Triumph shared in this chapter inspire you? Why is it important for you to share your story of triumph?

Write out your own story of triumph in your journal.

Review: Journey to the Sunrise

Discover the wonder of your loving family and friends cheering you on.

Realize that finish lines inspire new goals and a new sense of potential in life.

Understand that life's changes will bring depth and unexpected beauty into your life, and you can begin to enjoy living in that space.

Steps on the Path

Crafting your new normal after loss takes practice in creating a new life pattern and then repeating that pattern.

What can you start doing?

How can you use what you have learned to help others?

Break down how you will achieve that goal into monthly, weekly, and daily tasks. Are you doing this?

How can you use what you have learned to help others?

Encouragement Tips

Get support as you move toward that goal. Finally, cross your finish line.

It's hard to think about what the next phase of your life will look like when you don't feel well.

Training for a race event will help you to feel better, clear your mind, and train you to accomplish your future goals.

This process is a practice, a discipline, a repeatable pattern. It does not depend upon your emotions.

One day, you will be able to say like Mishael did, "If I can do this, I can do anything!"

When you feel stronger and have established a pattern for moving forward, life opens up into your Great Adventure!

Pray, asking God to help you begin to enjoy where you are in this journey now as you move from being a victim to becoming a victor. Write your prayers here.

Speak Life
Cross Your Finish Line

(Read Out Loud)

I have arrived at the Okavango at just the right time. I celebrate my Victory and the Victory of my Teammates! We have come a long way! We drink deeply of the fresh water, now spilling into the tremendous basin, shaped like a giant hand, reminding us of God's provision. The flood- waters are rising, and the basin steadily fills. We rest and refresh ourselves, because this is just the beginning. The light of dawn is peeking over the horizon. It is the start of a New Day. I have come far, but my journey isn't over yet.

Food for Thought

Week 7: Journal Entries

Movie time! Take a few hours and watch the movie Secretariat. When watching the film, be mindful of how the process to success wasn't easy. We each have a race to run—let's get moving! ~ Mishael

Day 1: Run Your Race

Have you crossed a finish line yet, such as a 5K, 10K, or sprint triathlon? Write about your triumph moment here.

Food for Thought

Week 7: Journal Entries

Day 2: Your Finish Line

Do you have a finish line to cross in the near future? What is that date?
Is there anything or anyone encumbering your training experience? What is distracting you from accomplishing your goal?

Food for Thought
Week 7: Journal Entries

Day 3: Distractions

What can you do to minimize or eliminate those distractions?

Food for Thought

Week 7: Journal Entries

Day 4: Win the Prize

What does it mean to you to run your race in life so as to win the prize? What does a life well lived look like for you in your circumstances?

Food for Thought

Week 7: Journal Entries

Day 5: Look Who Is Watching You

Whom do you want to most influence with your life choices?
Who is counting on you to thrive in your life so that they can thrive in theirs?

Live Your Legacy

Week 8

Worksheet for Step Seven
Live Your Legacy

Read Chapters 20-22
180 Your Life from Tragedy to Triumph

Chapter 20: Cleaning the Bricks and Crafting Your Legacy

You will need a Bible, a pen, and a notebook. (You can use this journal, but you may need additional pages to really write out your stories.)

Read: Cleaning the Bricks

> *"If we take the broken bricks of our lives, clean them, and use them to rebuild our own mon- ument to hope, maybe we would build something that could help others, as we also choose to honor our past. The problem is, we will keep on stumbling over the bricks left over from our previous hurts, unless we find a way to clean them up and put them to use. In the process of getting the van ready to sell, God taught me a thing or two about cleaning the mess, reclaiming a sealed space, restoring the damage, and then refueling my dreams."*

How did this story of cleaning the bricks help you in your grief journey?

Share your thoughts on Mishael's story about cleaning up her van.

> *"To reclaim the space, I had to open the van to the sunshine, reveal the wasp nests, get my helpful neighbor to spray them, knock the nests down, and stomp them."*

This symbolizes what?

> *"Next, I needed a new battery."*

This symbolizes what?

> *"Next, the vehicle needed to get some intensive repairs so the mechanical parts could function."*

This symbolizes what?

"Then, I gave it a new identity and a new outlook."

This symbolizes what?

One of the ways to "clean the bricks" of dreams that have been bombed is to tell your story. Write down the stories as they come to you, both celebratory and soulful. There doesn't have to be an order to it. Your stories become part of your family's oral traditions and help to build a kind of narrative identity for your family.

Start this process today. That is why you needed an extra notebook, a pen, and your Bible. Write a Bible verse that has helped you in your grief journey across the bottom of your notebook or on the first page of the journal section for this week.

In crafting your own lasting legacy, you will find that telling your story is vital to transforming your trials into triumph. Whether you paint your story, write your story, or find some other way to share your story, there is an eventual, surprising release and joy in giving purpose to the pain.

However you choose to express yourself, it's healthy to express what you are feeling. Writing or painting or any sort of healthy artistic expression gives your mind time to process what has happened.

Our stories have the power to inspire others, and helping others is another powerful source of joy and healing for our hearts and minds. When our pain has a purpose, we can focus on how telling our story may help someone else, and that effort gives us joy in the present moment.

Create a page in your notebook with bricks. Whatever comes to mind, write it in a brick. Do not worry about any kind of order. You will just use these to go back to later to begin to write your grief journey story.

Mishael said,

> *"Writing out my discoveries on this grief journey has been an excellent way to 'write myself well.' Over time, I can see the trajectory of God's faithfulness, even in the most painful circumstances. This book has been a most difficult thing for me to write, but it has also brought incredible healing by giving purpose to my grief journey. It has transformed our family's trials into a helpful triumph."*

Whether you paint your story, write your story, or find some other way to share your story, there is an eventual, surprising release and joy in giving purpose to the pain.

> *"Your pain is part of the living legacy of your family. The choices you make with your pain can craft your family narrative far beyond your days here on earth."*

Review: Journey to the Sunrise

Discover the steps it will take to rehabilitate neglected memories and relationships.

Realize that you will keep on stumbling over the bricks left over from your previous hurts unless you find a way to clean them up and put them to use.

Understand that if you take the broken bricks of your life, clean them, and use them to rebuild your own monument to hope, that becomes a movement of hope. You can build something that could help others, as you also choose to honor your past. Start small; start with just helping someone on your Team.

What part of your grief journey testimony will help others honor their past?

Pray and ask God to help you clean up the broken bricks of your life and use them to rebuild your own monument to hope as you move forward, filling your journal with your testimonies. Write your prayers here.

Speak Life
Live Your Legacy

(Read Out Loud)

The Okavango Basin has filled to overflowing and I am being refreshed. Now the fresh waters spill their borders and begin to fill the dry, ancient riverbeds. The water is streaming into the desert, rising with volume, heading to pools and watering holes to revive life all around it. Like those refreshing waters, my heart overflows with streams of kindness that surge forward to help and refresh others in their loss. I will look for these opportunities of service, as they will become a spring of life within me. This is part of my Living Legacy. The sun is rising, and the landscape of my life is transforming right before my eyes.

You may draw the bricks for your stories here. Put the name of each of your memorable stories in each brick. The order doesn't matter. Now get your notebook or computer and start writing these stories out one by one. These bricks will eventually become part of your monument to hope. They become part of your legacy narrative to your loved ones and family.

Food for Thought

Week 8: Journal Entries

The choices you make and how you live your life are not only about you. These choices become your legacy that lives on in the lives of those you love. ~ Mishael

Day 1: Cleaning the Bricks

What does the story of cleaning the bricks mean to you?
Paint a picture with your words: What did your life look like after loss?

Food for Thought

Week 8: Journal Entries

Day 2: Your Monument to Hope

How can you best put those bricks of loss to good use? What does your monument to hope look like?

Food for Thought

Week 8: Journal Entries

Day 3: Crafting Your Legacy

Who has most influenced your life? What is inspirational about this person?

Food for Thought

Week 8: Journal Entries

Day 4: Influencing Others

How do you want to influence others with your life choices?

Food for Thought

Week 8: Journal Entries

Day 5: Get Out of Your Own Head

How can you leverage your pain into inspirational purpose?

Make some time to help others—for example, working at a Habitat for Humanity build or volunteering at a soup kitchen.

Get out of your head for a while and see the lives of others.

Describe where you volunteered, the experience, and how you felt.

Unveil Your Triumph

Week 9

Worksheet for Step 8
Unveil Your Triumph

Read Chapter 23
180 Your Life from Tragedy to Triumph

Chapter 23: Flood of Love and Woman of Valor

An excellent wife, who can find? For her worth is far above jewels. (Proverbs 31:10 NASB)

Mishael shares in the book,

> *The description of the perfect woman in Proverbs 31 used to frustrate me. The Proverbs woman was the perfect wife. I wondered, "How can I ever measure up to this married super- woman? Does my marital status determine my worth?" But then I began to look at her more closely. In various translations of the Bible, the Proverbs woman is referred to as a "perfect wife," an "excellent wife," a "truly good wife," a "capable wife," and a "competent wife." But other versions speak only of an "excellent woman," a "virtuous woman." In the Orthodox Jewish Bible, this perfect female is called aishet chayil, a "woman of valor."[1]*

What does "valor" mean? "Great courage in the face of danger, especially in battle. The medals are awarded for acts of valor. Synonyms are: bravery, courage, pluck, nerve, daring, fearlessness, audacity, boldness, dauntlessness, stout-heartedness, heroism, backbone, spirit, (informal) guts, true grit, spunk, moxie;" "Strength of mind or spirit that enables a person to encounter danger with firmness: personal bravery."[2]

Who is a "woman of valor?" She need not be a wife. In fact, according to Gordon-Bennet, a Judaism expert, the one woman in the Bible who is specifically called *aishet chayil*—the one woman who fulfills all the many qualities that make for the perfect, excellent, virtuous, competent woman—was a widow.[3] According to Gordon-Bennet, "One reference to a woman of valor appears in the Book of Ruth, which tells the story of the convert Ruth and her journey with her mother-in-law, Naomi and marriage to Boaz. When Boaz refers to Ruth as an *aishet chayil*, it makes her the only woman in all the books of the Bible to be referred to as such."

Even more, Ruth earns the title of "woman of valor" because she insists on supporting her mother-in-law, Naomi. Without Ruth, Naomi's story is tragic. Naomi has been called a female version of Job because of the trials she undergoes after she moves with her husband and sons away from their famine-stricken home. Then her husband dies, leaving her a widow, and dependent on her two sons. Her sons marry, but then they also die. Naomi now has no means to support herself, and no protectors—she is too old to have more sons, and too old for a new husband (she says this). So she sends her daughters-in-law back to their own families, because they at least are young enough to remarry. Ruth refuses to abandon her mother-in-law. She vows to stay with Naomi, saying, *"whither thou goest, I will go; and where thou lodgest, I will lodge: thy people shall be my people, and thy God my God: Where thou diest, will I die, and there will I be buried."* (Ruth 1:16-17 KJV)

---

[1] *In order, the references come from these versions of the Bible: ERV, ESV, CEV, CJB, CEB, AMP, KJV, OJB.*

[2] *"Valor." Google.com. N.d.; "Valor." Miriam-webster.com. 2015. Web. 12/21/2015.*

[3] *Chaviva Gordon-Bennet. "What Is Aishes Chayel?" Judaism.about.com. 2015. Web. 12/21/2015.*

Ruth's biblical vow to be part of Naomi's Team has endured through the ages as a beautiful love pledge, often used in wedding ceremonies today.

Ruth, the woman of valor, is a widow without a job or a place to live, supporting her mother-in-law, another widow in need. Eventually, Ruth marries Boaz and gives birth to Obed, bringing honor to Naomi also. Obed later becomes the grandfather of King David, and great-grandfather to the eminently wise King Solomon.

> ***Ruth is an example for all those determined to journey through grief with faith and perseverance, and in so doing, transform their tragedy into triumph.***

Review: Journey to the Sunrise

Discover what being a woman of valor means to you.

Realize that you are not a survivor, but a warrior.

Understand that you can move forward on this journey, crafting the next chapters of your life, grounded in peace and valor.

Think of the story of Ruth you read about in this session's lesson and use her example to help you with these questions.

Describe what being "a woman of valor" means to you.

Describe what it means to not just be a survivor, but a warrior.

How did Ruth's story help you better understand that you can move forward on this journey, crafting the next chapters of your life, grounded in peace and valor?

What hope does Ruth's story give you that her journey did not end with loss?

Many Jewish scholars consider the widow Ruth to be the original Woman of Valor. As such, she is considered the Greatest, Wisest Matriarchal Leader on the journey through the desert of grief into the flood lands of transformation and triumph.

How have you changed during this process?

Have you had a moment when God has flooded your landscape of loss with love, refreshing your heart with His Spirit? Describe your experience.

Read over a traditional Jewish translation of Proverbs 31:10-31

Certificate of Completion

_____

this_____ day of_____ in the year_____

has completed the
180 Your Life Journey to Renewal
and is hereby confirmed to be a

Woman of Valor

A Woman of Valor who can find? For her price is far above rubies.

~Proverbs 31:10

A woman of valor who can find? She is far more precious than jewels. The heart of her husband trusts in her, and he will have no lack of gain. She does him good, and not harm, all the days of her life.

She seeks wool and flax, and works with willing hands.

She is like the ships of the merchant; she brings her food from afar.

She rises while it is yet night and provides food for her household and portions for her maidens.

She considers a field and buys it; with the fruit of her hands she plants a vineyard. She dresses herself with strength and makes her arms strong.

She perceives that her merchandise is profitable. Her lamp does not go out at night.

She puts her hands to the distaff, and her hands hold the spindle.

She opens her hand to the poor and reaches out her hands to the needy.

She is not afraid of snow for her household, for all her household are clothed in scarlet. She makes bed coverings for herself; her clothing is fine linen and purple.

Her husband is known in the gates when he sits among the elders of the land.

She makes linen garments and sells them; she delivers sashes to the merchant. Strength and dignity are her clothing, and she laughs at the time to come.

She opens her mouth with wisdom, and the teaching of kindness is on her tongue. She looks well to the ways of her household and does not eat the bread of idleness. Her children rise up and call her blessed; her husband also, and he praises her: "Many women have done excellently, but you surpass them all."

Charm is deceitful, and beauty is vain, but a woman who fears the LORD is to be praised. Give her of the fruit of her hands, and let her works praise her in the gates.[4]

How do you think you can incorporate virtues of valor in your daily walk? In the walk of your family?

What does it mean to you that "charm is deceitful, and beauty vain, but a woman who fears the Lord is to be praised"?

---

[4] *John J. Parsons. "Eschet Chayil—Praising a Woman of Valor." hebrew4christians.com. N.d. Web. 12/21/2015.*

Steps on the Path

Mishael writes,

> *"It has been said that grief unveils your true self. I hope that through this journey your heart has changed and is better able to handle life's challenges. You have done the hard work, committed to the quest, braved the fires of pain, pushed through the drought of the soul, and have emerged empowered, strengthened, and wiser. You are now becoming a leader and a warrior of the spirit, trained to defend, mentor, and protect those who are still hurting. Leading others to the flood lands that refresh our spirits and heralding a movement of hope."*

Describe the part of Mishael's story that has encouraged you the most.

Describe a moment of valor, of being strong in the face of difficulty you have experienced in your own life.

You are not just a survivor, but a warrior, a Woman of Valor.

Mishael's prayer over you:

> *This is my prayer of valor for you as you forge ahead into the next chapters of your life. May you be clothed with dignity and strength, and laugh without fear of the future. May you work industriously, opening your hands to the poor and putting your time and efforts to promote honor and kindness over the fleeting activity of charm and vanity. May grief so transform you that your true self is revealed, your very best self. May this legacy of strength cause those you love, mentor, and influence to rise up and call you blessed.*

> *May you move forward on this journey, crafting the next chapters of your life, grounded in peace and valor. May you use your strength, forged in the fire of grief, to help those on your path, standing shoulder to shoulder with your Team, moving forward as an army of hope.*

Speak Life
Unveil Your Triumph

(Read Out Loud)

My heart has changed and is better able to handle life's challenges. I am committed to the quest of a renewed life. I will leverage my loss to help lead others, knowing I am a warrior of the spirit, trained to defend, mentor, and protect those who are still hurting.

I will be clothed with dignity and strength. I will laugh without fear of the future. I will work industriously, opening my hands to the poor, and promote honor and kindness over the fleeting activity of charm and vanity. May this legacy of strength cause those I love, mentor, and influence to rise up and call me blessed.

Food for Thought

Week 9: Journal Entries

God's timing coupled with your intuition and obedience is a winning combination. ~ Mishael

Day 1: God Moment

Has there been a "God moment" when you knew you had a divine appointment, when you felt God was evident in your circumstances? Describe what happened.

Food for Thought

Week 9: Journal Entries

Day 2: God Nudges

Don't be afraid to move when the Spirit leads. Because when God asks us to do something, it's timely. Has God been nudging you to do something to step out in faith? Describe what you feel that nudge may be about.

Food for Thought

Week 9: Journal Entries

Day 3: God Directives

God's directives are timely—meaning, your timely obedience can activate God's plan for you. What can you do this week to obey God?

Food for Thought

Week 9: Journal Entries

Day 4: Treasure Hunt

If God knows me and cares for me, then I don't have to be constantly vigilant against unknown danger. Go on a treasure hunt for verses that speak to you about God's faithfulness. List your five favorite verses here.

Food for Thought

Week 9: Journal Entries

Day 5: God's Faithfulness

Jesus has given His life for you because He loves you with an everlasting love. Reflect on the last several months.
What are your thoughts now on God as a Heavenly Husband? List ways that God has been faithful to you during this journey.

Week 10

Worksheet: The Celebration Dinner

Read Chapter 24
180 Your Life from Tragedy to Triumph

Chapter 24: Celebration Dinner

Mishael shares,

> *"As we look over the lush African veldt, once a desert which now teems with life, let us set up camp and enjoy rest and refreshment. After you take a dip in the pool—mind the hippos—we will relax at a feast honoring your arrival. In the cool of the evening, under a breezy tent, (or dining room), I want to raise a toast in your honor because you have come a long way. Remember our verse from the beginning of our journey?"*

Forget the former things; do not dwell on the past. See, I am doing a new thing! Now it springs up; do you not perceive it? I am making a way in the wilderness and streams in the wasteland. (Isaiah 43:18-19)

This verse is not about forgetting our loved ones who have passed on, but can signify to us our embrace of the transformational power of God on our grief journey. In Judaism, eight is the number of new beginnings, which is why the *180 Your Life* journey has eight steps to travel from tragedy to triumph. This is meant to signify your journey of new beginnings in your life after loss.

Honor God in Your Life: Part of the author's journey was realizing that God was indeed her Heavenly Husband. We are never alone. God is always with us. Let's meditate on these verses:

For your Maker is your husband—the LORD Almighty is his name, the Holy One of Israel is your Redeemer; he is called the God of all the earth. (Isaiah 54:5 NIV)

No longer will they call you Deserted, or name your land Desolate. But you will be called Hephzibah, and your land Beulah; for the LORD will take delight in you, and your land will be married. (Isaiah 64:4 NIV)

When they walk through the Valley of Weeping, it will become a place of refreshing springs. The autumn rains will clothe it with blessings. (Psalm 84:6 NIV)

Read the Jewish Wedding Ketubah, or wedding contract between a husband and his wife. Fill in your name to remind yourself of your commitment to Jesus and His commitment to you as your Heavenly Husband.

Honor Your Loved One with The Headstone Service

We've learned about a Jewish tradition called a "Headstone Service," also known as an "Unveiling Service." This ceremony typically takes place at the end of the twelfth month of mourning. This is when a headstone is installed at the gravesite as a monument to the loved one who has passed on. This service focuses on honoring and celebrating the life of the person who has passed and the lives of those who have been changed by this passing.

*You have been saying your own kind of liturgy of renewal for the last twelve months, but today, recite a traditional prayer that honors your loved one and affirms life as your life moves forward. Read the prayer out loud and say the name of your loved one in the blanks. **(These prayers are shared by Rabbi Janet Madden / Complete Ceremony).***

"…It is an ancient Jewish custom to erect a *matzevah* – which does not mean 'gravestone,' 'tombstone' or 'marker.' The literal translation of *matzevah* is 'monument.' We erect a *matzevah* in memory and in honor of our beloved dead – a tradition that comes from Jacob, who placed a monument on the grave of his beloved Rachel.

"(Insert your loved ones' name): Our purpose in having a *matzevah* is to recall what is sacred and eternal about _____'s life.

"We have gathered to mark this time in the life of _____ 's friends and family and to make this new memory of coming together in _____'s honor to witness and support one another and to honor _____.

"Unveiling is a formal presentation and public presentation. It is the act of beginning a new phase. It also affords us a glimpse of Mystery: to unveil _____'s *matzevah* is to reveal and disclose how much we miss _____ , what has happened in our own lives since _____ 's death, and to again experience the thinning of the veils between the worlds."[5]

After saying a prayer of dedication, take your decorated rock and place it by the photo of your loved one, saying your loved one's name out loud and lighting a candle near the photo.

Honor Your Journey

Have eight unlit candles available, one for each step of your journey, honoring each step you have taken in the face of tragedy on your quest toward triumph.

Step One–Empower Your Ground Zero: *I will not lie down in the Desert of Grief. That is not my destiny. I am on a quest. Though the grasses have browned, the ground has cracked, and the night is full of the unknown, I sense a presence. I ask God to show me the way to the flood lands of the soul. I rise, taking one step and then another, moving forward into the night, pressing on toward the waters of renewal and the light of day.*

---

[5] *Rabbi Janet Madden. "HaKamat HaMatzevah: An Unveiling Ceremony." Ritualwell.org. Reconstructionist Rabbinical College, 2015. Web. 12/21/2015.*

Step Two–Forge Your Team: *As I press into this journey, I will join others who understand my loss around the campfire, so we may strengthen one another for this quest. We will come together in trust and confidence, for protection, friendship, and renewal. We will speak hope, speak purpose, and speak life to one another. Though the plains are arid, we take refreshment at a watering hole, encouraging one another, content to know we are not alone.*

Step Three–Train Your Mind: *I have met the constrictor, which stealthily coiled around me while I grieved, almost imperceptible, threatening to constrict my movements and even my very breath. With courage, asking for God's help, I will take conscious steps to firmly unwrap its coils from my life, minimizing chaos and creating healthy boundaries, as I purpose to create calm and peace in my home and my mind.*

Step Four–Train Your Body: *Even when the sands were hot, I have purposed to strengthen my body through conscious, healthy choices in what I eat and drink. I commit to an exercise schedule in a supportive, accountable Team, with a definite finish line, in order to accomplish my health goals. I will be open to asking God to be my coach.*

Step Five–Train Your Spirit: *I have continued to press into the heart of grief when it feels most dry. I have chosen gratitude, forgiveness, prayer, kindness, and generosity of soul in the most parched of circumstances. Even when the grasses around me were flaming hot with the heat of loss, I have purposed to press on, seeking God in prayer, worship, and Bible reading as an act of will. By the grace of God, I will not run from the desert, but instead will make positive choices in the midst of my tragedy, practicing spiritual discipline, which will yield a mighty harvest in due time. I will follow the ancient paths back to God, trusting and believing that the mighty floodwaters of the Spirit will come as refreshment from the hand of God.*

Step Six–Cross Your Finish Line: *I have arrived at the Okavango at just the right time. I celebrate my Victory and the Victory of my Teammates. We have come a long way. We drink deeply of the fresh water, now spilling into the tremendous basin, shaped like a giant hand, reminding us of God's provision. The floodwaters are rising, and the basin steadily fills. We rest and refresh ourselves because this is just the beginning. The light of dawn is peeking over the horizon. It is the start of a New Day. I have come far, but my journey isn't over yet.*

Step Seven–Live Your Legacy: *The Okavango Basin has filled to overflowing and I am being refreshed. Now the fresh waters spill their borders and begin to fill the dry, ancient riverbeds. The water is streaming into the desert, rising with volume, heading to pools and watering holes to revive life all around it. Like those refreshing waters, my heart overflows with streams of kindness that surge forward to help and refresh others in their loss. I will look for these opportunities of service, as they will become a spring of life within me. This is part of my Living Legacy. The sun is rising, and the landscape of my life is transforming right before my eyes.*

Step Eight–Unveil Your Triumph: *My heart has changed and is better able to handle life's challenges. I am committed to the quest of a renewed life. I will leverage my loss to help lead others knowing I am a warrior of the spirit, trained to defend, mentor, and protect those who are still hurting. I will be clothed with dignity and strength. I will laugh without fear of the future. I will work industriously, opening my hands to the poor, and promote honor and kindness over the fleeting activity of charm and vanity. May this legacy of strength cause those I love, mentor, and influence to rise up and call me blessed.*

Describe the growth you have seen during your journey.

How have you "adventurized" your life through reading the *180 Your Life* book and going through this study on your transformation from tragedy to triumph journey?

Receive this blessing from Mishael:

Not only do you arrive at the dawn of a new day, the rising of the sun also happens within you, shining ever brighter in your life as you become your best version of the person God created you to be. You are beloved and fit into a Master Plan.

My prayer for you is that, through your own journey, you have transformed from within, no longer wandering in the night of the soul, but rather radiating like the rising sun. My prayer is that, in time, hope shines through you, by your life's example, as an ever-brightening dawn of a new day. Let your goal be a life that was transformed by grief, from pain to purpose, from tragedy to triumph.

My hope is that you are refreshed and renewed, and that your new growth yields the jeweled fruits of love, patience, perseverance, forgiveness, joy, kindness, generosity, and peace. May these super-fruits nourish and empower your spirit as you have reclaimed your life, cleared your ground, pressed into grief and faith, spoken to your bones, nourished your body, and started the Divine Conversation. I pray that this process has helped you find the source of Life-Giving Water. You have braved the cold night of the soul, forged your Team, unwrapped the python of constriction, and strengthened and disciplined your body. Though parched, you pressed into the desert, determined to cross your finish line, purposed to rebuild and refresh others, and now you emerge triumphant.

The hot fires of grief have transformed you into a Woman of Valor. A warrior, nay, a Band of Warriors.

This journey doesn't end here. My prayer is that you move forward as a supportive community. Keep working the steps, mentoring newcomers, and moving forward together. As the African Proverb says, "We go faster alone but farther together."

Each person heals at her own pace. This is a wonderful step, the beginning of a life you love. Mishael did not feel fully *recovered* in a year's time after her loss. That's okay. Commit to working these steps as a lifestyle. Grief, like the overflowing Okavango, is cyclical. There will be times of refreshment and times of dryness. Now, you know what to do. You have a plan and a community. You have discovered that grief isn't something to be raced through once you are in it, because grief has the potential to be powerfully transformative. If you let it, grief can be the path to your purpose.

Pray and ask God to help you as you continue your journey from tragedy to triumph.

Food for Thought

Week 10: Closing Journal Entries

I am so honored that you have taken the time to allow God to transform you as you continue to move toward greater triumphs in your life. This is how you mindfully craft a life you love, a life that honors God and helps others. Ponder the last year and reflect on where you have been and where you are going in your next chapter. This journey is cyclical, taking you to greater awareness every year you work these steps. It's how I live my life, and I hope it's helped you in yours. ~ Mishael

Day 1: Bringing the Flowers Forward

Our life can be like a garden, and we can let the beauty of the past *coexist* in healthy ways with the beauty of the present.
What does this look like in your life?

Food for Thought

Week 10: Journal Entries

Day 2: Reflect on Your Journey

Go back and look at the goals you set for your life at the beginning of this journal. Did you accomplish your goals?
List the goals you accomplished.

Food for Thought

Week 10: Journal Entries

Day 3: New Directions

What is your new goal for the coming year?

Food for Thought

Week 10: Journal Entries

Day 4: Design Your Plan

How will you accomplish this goal?

Food for Thought

Week 10: Journal Entries

Day 5: Join In

Will you choose to participate in the *180 Your Life* program again in the upcoming year, maybe even helping to mentor someone new on the grief path?

Dear Sister, Thank you for taking the time to be mindful about your journey. I hope that this experience has helped you heal, dream, and move forward with purpose into a life you love.

My prayer for you comes from Isaiah 45:8 (NET Bible) O sky, rain down from above!
Let the clouds send down showers of deliverance! Let the earth absorb it so salvation may grow, and deliverance may sprout up along with it.
I, the Lord, create it.

May God bless your healing journey and may you turn to others and comfort them with the comfort you have been given by Him. Your healing gives purpose to my own loss, and in doing so, helps us all work together to become a living monument to hope. Thank you for taking this journey with me. I hope that you don't stop here but continue onward. I still work these steps in my life every year. Each year brings new discoveries, new adventures, and new refreshment. Move forward as a warrior, forged in the fires of grief, trained to protect and guide in hope those who are new on this transformational journey.

Be the Light,

Mishael

Disclaimer

A mystery is a phenomenon that you cannot fully understand because you were not there. So it is with Jason's passing. My best friend and husband died of carbon monoxide poisoning in his car. His death was first deemed a suicide, and, violently disbelieving that conclusion while I was pregnant and grieving, I called a coroner's inquest as soon as possible after my husband passed away. I presented information to the coroner for months and ultimately presented enough doubt that Jason's death was later deemed an accident on his death certificate. But the police investigator who first deemed his death a suicide in his police report would never change his conclusion from suicide to accidental. When Jason died, I was surprised to discover there was a two-year suicide clause in our life insurance policy. We'd had the policy for 3.5 years. Therefore, my husband's cause of death didn't affect what our insurance policy provided for our family, but the determination of his cause of death mattered to me greatly. That is why I fought so hard for Jason's death to be deemed an accident, because that is what I wanted to believe. Then, three years after my husband's death, better able to handle this grief, I went back to the place where Jason died. I had never been there before. I investigated the facts of his passing like a journalist would. I spoke at length with the first responder, a park ranger. I investigated the campsite where he died. I spoke for hours with the police investigator who was at the scene of his death. I even reviewed all the photos that were taken. That's when I finally understood and believed that the police investigator was correct about Jason's cause of death, and I started to process my late husband's passing as a suicide. I was heartsick when I started to accept this conclusion, though it made logical sense to me. Ultimately, I decided it was best to give my daughters the opportunity to heal in truth throughout their childhood with access to skilled grief professionals. Our choice was not to hide from exploring the truth as a family. My daughters and I now process Jason's death, with extreme love and compassion, as a suicide, and so that is why this book reflects that journey.

Author Bios

Mishael Porembski: Southeastern Emmy-winning documentarian and twenty-year network news veteran, was catapulted into intense grief by her husband's suicide. To help her overcome the resulting depression, anger, and despair, Mishael turned to her faith in Jesus and, over time, discovered a healthy path to a new God-adventure. Now a widowed mom, life coach, speaker, and author, Mishael encourages grieving families to healthfully craft a life they love and leave a lasting legacy of hope. She founded a nonprofit, Widow Strong, an active clinically proven, Biblically-based support group movement for widows and their children.

Dr. Larry Keefauver: Contributing author, Dr. Keefauver is married to Judi Keefauver, and together he and his wife have been in ministry for over 40 years. Both have extensive experience in counseling and mentoring. Their three adult children are married, are actively living for the Lord, and are parenting seven grandchildren. Judi and Larry have traveled internationally, leading seminars and conferences on family, marriage, parenting, church leadership, and spiritual growth. They have an international TV program, Family Forum, seen throughout Taiwan, China, Korea, and on the Internet through GoodTV.

Dr. Larry Keefauver, with degrees from the University of Pennsylvania and Texas Christian University, is professionally and educationally trained in pastoral counseling, and Judi is a registered nurse. Best-selling family books include: Lord, I Wish My Family Would Get Saved; The 77 Irrefutable Truths of Parenting (with Judi); Proactive Parenting—The Early Years; The 77 Irrefutable Truths of Marriage (with Judi); Lord, I Wish My Teenager Would Talk With Me; and Lord, I Wish My Husband Would Pray with Me. Judi's devotional book for women is Be.

With over 2.5 million books worldwide in 12 languages, Dr. Keefauver is the noted author of Inviting God's Presence, When God Doesn't Heal Now, Experiencing the Holy Spirit, The 77 Irrefutable Truths of Ministry, Hugs for Grandparents, Hugs for Heroes, Commanding Angels— Invoking the Standing Orders, From the Oval Office: Prayers of the Presidents, The 77 Irrefutable Truths of Prayer and Friend to Friend.

He edited the bestselling through-the-Bible-in-one-year curriculum—What the Bible is All About (Gospel Light). Other adult curricula include Making Love Last Forever (with Gary Smalley), Truth Matters (with Josh McDowell), and The Seasons of a Man's Life (Patrick Morley), all with Lifeway Press.

Dr. Keefauver was ordained by The Christian Church (Disciples of Christ, 1973) and credentialed by the Open Bible Faith Fellowship of Canada (since 2000). He has served 31 years in the local church as associate, executive, and senior pastor. He founded Your Ministry Counseling Services in 2000 and has served as President and Executive Director for over twenty-five years. He has written extensively for CfaN, Charisma Media, HarperCollins/Nelson, Simon and Schuster, Gospel Light, Bridge Logos, and numerous other publishers.

Dr. Keefauver has written extensively for Christian magazines and is a contributing editor and writer for *Ministry Today, Kairos,* and *Harvest Times*. Dr. Keefauver serves as Senior Editor and Author Coach for Xulon Press and has edited and ghostwritten hundreds of books and curricula over the past decade for Christian leaders in the Church, business, arts and media, and medical/ nutrition fields. A partial list is as follows:

Josh McDowell, The Father Connection and Truth Matters
Dr. Gary Smalley, Making Love Last Forever and How to Win Your Husband Back
Rod Parsley, No More Crumbs, No Dry Season, The Day Before Eternity
Daniel Kolenda, This Is That
CfaN, Harvest Joy
Editor, The Holy Spirit Encounter Bible (Creation House) Dr. Leeland Jones, Wholeness
Bishop David Evans, Dare to be a Man
Dr. Keith Johnson, The Confidence Solution, The LQ Solution
Winston Nunes, Driven by the Spirit

And many more.

Editor Bio:

Bridget T. Heneghan, Ph.D.: Dr. Bridget Heneghan is an editor, teacher, and sometime triathlete in Marietta, Georgia. She earned her doctorate in English and began her career as a writing instructor at Vanderbilt University, later moving to Atlanta and teaching at Georgia Institute of Technology. Bridget has authored articles and reviews, as well as an interdisciplinary literary and archeological study, *Whitewashing America: Material Culture and Race in Antebellum America*. Behind the scenes, she edits and reviews professional, academic, and popular manuscripts and instructs students in the beauty of a well-placed comma and a well-turned phrase.

Consider exploring our 12-month series with your small group! There are additional videos that highlight practical steps as you journey forward and craft a life you love. This process takes time and with practice, can become the blueprint for your lifestyle moving forward!

Other books from the 180 Your Life series

180 Your Life from Tragedy to Triumph: A Woman's Grief Guide

180 Your Life New Beginnings: 10-Week Facilitator's Guide for Small Group Study

180 Your Life New Beginnings: 10-Week Video Series

180 Your Life from Tragedy to Triumph: 12-Month Facilitator's Guide

180 Your Life from Tragedy to Triumph: 12-Month Personal Study Guide & Journal

180 Your Life from Tragedy to Triumph: 12-Month Video Series

Learn more at 180YourLife.com

*Proceeds from our **180 Your Life** print and video grief empowerment curricula help support our sister nonprofit, Widow Strong. Learn more at WidowStrong.com*